OCT 1 2 2005

61727376

Quit Smoking the Easy Way

D0800112

PROPERTY
OF THE
FARGO PUBLIC LIBRARY

Lulu Inc.
www.lulu.com

Copyright © 2005 by Sallie Stone.
All rights reserved.

No part of this book may be reproduced in any
form or by any electronic or mechanical means
including information storage and retrieval
systems without permission in writing from the
publisher, except by a reviewer who may quote
brief passages in a review.

Cover design by Hock Ng of
www.eproductcover.com

613.85
S879
c.1

Table of Contents

Introduction

In this book we will be reviewing the various methods to quit smoking. Some are well known techniques, some are not; but the purpose of this book is to introduce people to the easy way to quit smoking.

It will be the subject of our last chapter. If you're anxious or curious to know what the easy method is, then you can read the last chapter first.

Our first chapter begins with a little known secret to aid in fighting off nicotine cravings with a product you can find in any drugstore or supermarket. What is it? Well I don't want to spoil the surprise. It is the topic of our first chapter.

If you're like me you have tried several times to quit with little success. I tried the patch, nicotine gum, and Zyban. I even tried this elaborate system of putting a pre-made piece of plastic, a filter on my cigarettes. The purpose of this device was to gradually reduce the amount of nicotine. Not a bad idea. These filters are still sold in drugstores today. While all these methods work people don't always have success with them. We will be discussing them in the coming chapters along with some little known but effective ways to quit. In this book you will finally have the information you need to quit smoking for good.

Foreword

Let's begin our journey together and find the best method for you to quit. Each chapter provides a way for you to have your victory and finally quit smoking for good.

You will be presented with all of the ways to quit smoking known to this author and finally be taught the easy way to quit smoking.

Cinnamon Gum

For thousands of years people have been using plants for medicine. In our time this practice is usually called Aroma therapy. In practicing Aroma therapy we can heal psychologically and physically.

Did you know that apple cider pills can be used to drain fat cells in the body? Or that Lavender essential oil used in a diffuser can calm your nerves and uplift your spirits.

Have you heard of smelling salts used to treat conditions? To calm your nerves you can put rock salt and Sandalwood essential oil in a small jar (mix it together before) and smell it to calm your nerves. Remember to put a top on the jar to preserve the freshness of the mixture.

Aroma therapy can calm your nerves but it isn't used widely to aid in quitting smoking. The use of plants as medicine is used throughout the world.

We've all seen the natural herbs advertised in drugstores, the internet and on t.v. to cleanse the body of nicotine and help with withdrawal symptoms. Well there's an easier way to fight nicotine cravings with one of God's plants. What is it? Cinnamon. Just chew Wrigley's Big Red Gum (cinnamon) to fight cravings of nicotine or any other harmful drug.

I met a woman who was very active in her church and she told me that cinnamon gum reduced cravings for nicotine. I tried it and found it to be true. She has introduced many people to this idea and has helped many people quit smoking. She also suggests writing notes to yourself around your house not to smoke.

How much I will Save

In addition to being a health hazard smoking costs a lot of money over time. Some people have to repaint or clean their white walls because there is a yellowish tint to the walls because of prolonged and continual exposure to cigarette smoke. Life insurance is more expensive for smokers than nonsmokers. Think of the money you will save in insurance costs alone. I have always found this next part to be fun. Let's figure out how much money you will save on smokes if you quit smoking.

How Much You will Save at 3.50 a Pack

Cigs Per Day	Cost per Month	Cost per Year
10	$52.50	$630.00
20	$105.00	$1260.00
30	$157.50	$1890.00
40	$210.00	$2520.00

Look in the chart and figure how much you spend on cigarettes a month. Don't forget you could be doing something else with that money. Here are some suggestions on how to spend the money you have saved. Of course, you will come up with your own ways to use the money.

- Save money for retirement in an IRA.

- Put the money in a college account for your children.

- Donate the money to your favorite charity.

- Go on an expensive vacation.

- Buy new clothes.

- Open a savings account or mutual fund.

- Join a health club.

- Sponsor a child in another country.

- Enroll in a yoga class or any class.

Jot down some ways you would like to spend the money you will save. Don't be afraid to write in your book. It's your book.

How I could spend the money I saved:

Relieving Withdrawal Cravings

The toughest part of quitting smoking is resisting the urge to smoke. The desire comes to smoke and immediately we light up another cigarette. Well, what if I told you that you could relieve that craving without smoking. Great, right? You can relieve that desire to smoke with a nicotine inhaler or nicotine gum on the spot. (You have to get a prescription from your doctor for a nicotine inhaler.)

The real way to relieve that craving is to find an alternative that is safe and natural. For instance you could meditate or pray until the desire leaves. A great meditation is counting your breath. This meditation can be found in *Awakening the Buddha Within* by Lama Surya Das. Lightly close your eyes. Count each inhale and exhale of breath until you get to ten and then start over. This will give you time to connect with your inner power. This meditation also works well if you are having trouble sleeping. Also, you could take one or two aspirin to help you sleep if the withdrawal symptoms are keeping you up at night.

With the easy way to quit smoking you won't be bothered with withdrawal symptoms. You will have little or no withdrawal symptoms because this method gets the nicotine out of your body a little at a time. If you do have an urge to smoke you can chew *Big Red* cinnamon Gum. Cinnamon gum fights nicotine cravings naturally and won't break the bank.

Triggers

We all have triggers that make us smoke. Sometimes we smoke because we are mad. Other times we smoke to celebrate, substituting a cigarette for a glass of champagne! We do this without thinking about it. It becomes automatic. In order to quit smoking, we need to identify these triggers so we won't be tempted to smoke when they arise. Most smokers have a lot in common when it comes to triggers. Here's a list of times in our lives that we smoke.

- Smoking because others are smoking.

- Smoking because we are happy.

- To relieve anger.

- To relieve anxiety.

- First thing in the morning.

- After a meal.

The Best Way to Quit Smoking: Fasting to Quit

Most quit smoking books, maybe all of them won't tell you what I'm about to tell you next. Fasting is one of the best methods to quit smoking, if not the best. It will give you what you need to quit smoking. A lot of us feel we can't quit smoking but we can. We fast so God will give us what we need to finally quit for good.

You should fast for three days to quit smoking. Fast on brown rice and water or carrot juice three days in a row. If you can't fast for three straight days fast one day a week for three weeks or as close together as possible. This method can be used cold turkey or with the method discussed in the last chapter; although I recommend cold turkey with this method.

I know this is a short chapter, but please don't let that make you think it is less important than any other chapter. This method will work for you, all you have to do is try.

The Ritual of Forgiveness

Smoking is a sin and should be viewed as such. Most books won't tell you this. They don't won't to make you feel bad or make you mad. I am telling you this because it was one of the reasons I quit smoking. I felt like my spiritual life was suffering as a result of my smoking.

It's not good to have a sin in your heart. This made me think about another important component for anyone's spiritual life called the Ritual of Forgiveness. This ritual frees your heart. First think about everyone who has ever wronged you. Make a list in your mind. Ask God or a saint in heaven to help you forgive each person and why you need to forgive them. Perform this ritual nightly until you have forgiven each individual.

You will find that your heart will become unburdened and you will forgive more easily. You will find that you are not only better off not smoking but that you are better off not holding resentment in your heart. Getting rid of any anger will help you to be a calmer person who is ready to quit smoking.

A Master's Word of Advice

Some people feel they are the exception to the rule that they are one of the only ones who can't quit. You will find that if you fast for three days you will be able to quit. A master once said to his disciple who was having a big problem that there was a hole in his net, and he just needed to find it. Well you have a hole in your net too. Just find that hole and you will be able to quit.

Why You Smoke

The only reason you smoke is because you smoked a cigarette previously. The last cigarette you smoked put nicotine in your body. This created the need for more nicotine. If you stopped smoking the need for nicotine would disappear.

After you quit smoking and the nicotine leaves your body you won't feel the need to smoke. This time period might seem like an eternity if you quit smoking cold turkey without any other method. This can be a recipe for disaster for some people.

I have provided two alternative methods in this book. They are fasting and tapering off. The tapering off method is the subject of our last chapter. It is the method I used to stop smoking along with fasting.

You're Ready to Quit

There are some signs in a smoker's life that he is ready to quit. Here are some signs that you're ready to quit.

-You have health concerns. You know you could die from smoking.

- You're tired of wasting money.

- You're tired of bad breath.

- Your clothes smell of smoke.

- Your walls will turn a yellowish tint.

- Your spiritual life is suffering.

- It's not convenient to smoke at work, church or school.

- People are nagging you to quit.

- Your family is tired of breathing in the fumes.

Write Down Some Reasons why you are ready to Quit

_____
_____
_____
_____
_____
_____
_____
_____
_____
_____

Seeking Balance

From a spiritual standpoint we can think of our bodies seeking balance when we smoke. Deepak Chopra, a well known meditation guru and world renowned author, says that smokers are very spiritual people. He has also said he has never met anyone who meditates or does yoga and smokes. Why is that? Well, they are not seeking balance through drugs or alcohol. They are getting a natural high and becoming one with their Creator and Higher Self.

One way we can heal our minds and connect with the divine source is through meditation. I highly recommend *Chi Kung Meditations: Taoist Inner Healing Exercises* with Ken Cohen. We can replace smoking with meditation in time if we are patient and have diligence. I highly recommend Hatha Yoga because in this practice you are becoming a very spiritual being that has inner peace and clarity of mind. Yoga is also good for people with mental diseases such as schizophrenia because the focus is on the body, not the mind.

Gum vs. Patch

Nicotine Gum is a good quit smoking aid. It is a behavior modification method. Instead of enjoying the pleasure of puffing, you are chewing gum to get nicotine in your body. While you are getting used to the idea of not smoking you still have nicotine in your body so you are not suffering physically. Psychologically you still crave the puffing, which is an oral fixation. This can be a psychological problem, however, and chewing gum helps an oral fixation.

The Patch is also available as a quit smoking aid. I don't think it is as effective as gum at controlling cravings because the medicine (nicotine) is slow released throughout the body, sometimes through a 24 hour period. I have tried this method, but found more success with the nicotine gum because I still had cravings while on the patch, and couldn't just put a piece of nicotine gum in my mouth.

Cold Turkey

Cold Turkey is a widely known method for quitting smoking, but not many people can actually do this, at least the first time. I guess you could say it's like ripping off a band-aid. It's better to get it over with.

It will take about three days for the nicotine to leave your body, and some say three weeks before the physical cravings end. Experts say you should not drink or eat sweets while quitting smoking because this can cause cravings for nicotine.

Drinking Chamomile tea can help calm your nerves through this process. If you use the cold turkey method you can chew Wrigley's *Big Red* (cinnamon) Gum to fight the cravings. You may also want to take Valerian pills found at the drugstore to calm your nerves. Please consult a physician before taking natural herbs like Valerian. Don't take natural herbs unless okayed by a doctor, and especially when you are taking prescription drugs because the herb or herbs can interfere with your medicine. Also remember 'all natural' on the label doesn't mean it's safe.

You might also want to consider getting a prescription for Wellbutrin, now called Zyban, for smokers. This drug reduces nicotine cravings. The first week you take the medicine you continue to smoke. This gives the body enough time to get used to the Zyban so it can work properly. Then you quit cold turkey.

Mind Changers

The subject of this chapter will be mind changers in the form of prayer. I honestly believe when you give up something that is not the will of God, he will replace it with something better. With that in mind I would like to teach you some prayers that are great replacements to smoking.

We'll start with a positive I AM affirmation. Say this mantra aloud if you can and repeat this ritual throughout the day.

I AM the peace and love of God. (9x)

Saying this mantra repeatedly will help you to find the peace and love of God. You will feel this peace and love inside of you. This prayer will work even better after you have quit smoking because you will be doing the will of God by quitting smoking, and he will bless you for it.

To find out more about positive I AM affirmations and prayer visit The Summit Lighthouse online at www.tsl.org.

Will I Gain Weight?

Some people gain weight when they quit smoking, usually no more than ten pounds. Gaining weight is a small price to pay for quitting smoking.

However, you don't need to gain weight while quitting smoking. It's not a good idea to replace smoking with overeating. There's no need for this. It won't make the withdrawal urges go away, and the extra weight won't make you happy.

If you do gain weight while quitting smoking, go on a diet. I think the best diet out there is Weight Watchers. Counting calories is not that hard to do. You can replace regular soda with diet soda. Small changes like that will make a world of difference if you do gain weight.

I didn't gain weight while quitting smoking because I went on a diet while I was quitting smoking. I just count calories and consume only about 1,200 calories a day. I will do this until I meet my weight goal. I keep a journal of how many calories I consume each day. I record my weight each day. Weigh yourself at the same time each day.

Rationalizations not to Quit

- You may feel that smoking helps you to eat less.

- Your friends and family smoke.

- It relaxes you.

- It helps you to deal with stress.

While all of these are valid reasons not to quit smoking they aren't good enough. There are too many reasons why you should quit. As I've said before smoking was ruining my spiritual life. That reason alone forced me to quit smoking and I've never regretted it since.

The Time Machine

Most of us who smoke would love to build a time machine. We would like to do this so we could go back to the first time we smoked and, not smoke that first one. This would be the better choice. We know this now, but it's too late. Well, we may not be able to build a time machine, but we can still quit and after several months it will be like we never smoked at all. Your physical desire to smoke will diminish, but it will take about two months for you to forget about smoking altogether. You will be as good as new after a couple of months.

Caffeine and Sugar

Caffeine is a stimulant and is not good for you. After you quit smoking you should consider limiting your caffeine intake or doing away with it altogether. You will feel more relaxed.

Sugar can also be considered a harmful substance that has no nutritional value. Too much sugar can lead to diabetes.

Support Groups and Workshops

Attending a support group may be what you need to quit smoking. There is a wonderful support group called Nicotine Anonymous. Nicotine Anonymous is a 12 step program similar to Alcoholics Anonymous. The program asks you to surrender your will to a higher power. You can find a meeting in your area by visiting www.nicotine-anonymous.org.

Some cities and towns have quit smoking workshops. These workshops often charge a fee. You may be able to find one at your local hospital.

Substitutes

Most quit smoking experts will tell you not to substitute anything with smoking. This includes candy and gum. Sugar can add to your craving for nicotine. I have advocated using cinnamon gum in a previous chapter, but that is because the cinnamon fights cravings. As a general rule however it is not good to substitute candy or gum. This can prolong the quitting process. Instead of quitting and just forgetting about smoking, you are prolonging the process. You don't need anything to replace smoking. You didn't need any replacement before you started smoking and your goal is to get back to the way you were before you started, or maybe new and improved.

Will my Personality Change?

Some people who want to quit smoking fear their personality will change. Well this is silly! In Buddhist philosophy there is a concept of impermanence. The feeling is that we are impermanent beings and that we change. The good part about being impermanent is that you can change for the better by stopping smoking.

Titration

Titration is the blending of sedatives with nicotine. Nicotine is a stimulant that gives you an up feeling. That explains why so many smokers feel they need to drink to relax. People often say that smoking is relaxing, but if that were the case they wouldn't find a need to drink, even though they smoke everyday. You will find that once you quit smoking, you are more relaxed because you won't have that stimulant in your body. It's like caffeine, it doesn't relax you it stimulates you. Don't use titration.

Withdrawal Symptoms

Smokers can experience withdrawal symptoms two - ten hours after smoking their last cigarette. These symptoms include:

- Anxiety.

- Mood Swings.

- Depression.

- Irritability.

- Disorientation.

- Anger.

- Hunger.

-Headaches.

That's why a medication like Zyban is helpful during the withdrawal stage because medication often relives these symptoms. I wanted to escape these symptoms; that's why I quit by tapering down and fasting.

Recognizing Poor Times to Quit

There are some poor times to quit. Stressful periods in your life are poor times to quit. You may be studying for a final exam or just experienced a breakup. This is not the right time to quit.

My method is so easy to use that you can begin to quit smoking the next day after you learn about it. This is not to say that you should make excuses not to quit. Waiting for a vacation won't work. You will get on your vacation and decide you don't want to ruin it by quitting smoking. The easy way to quit smoking is to taper down.

The Easy Way to Quit Smoking: Tapering Down

Well, you made it to the last chapter. I hope you found the previous information helpful to determine which method of quitting smoking you prefer.

The easy way to quit is new and revolutionary. You will quit smoking gradually with this method, and eliminate the suffering that occurs with cold turkey. The plan is simple; all you do is take away one cigarette a day until you are left with none.

First determine how many cigarettes you smoke a day. Let's say you're a heavy smoker and you smoke two packs a day. That's 40 cigarettes. On the first day you start the easy way you will smoke 39 cigarettes, the second day 38 cigarettes, on the fourth day 37 cigarettes. It will take you 39 days to get just one cigarette for the day. The next day you smoke none. Now what have you done really? Cut back? No, you have gradually taken the nicotine out of your body and you have given yourself ample time to get used to not smoking because you have done it in a gradual pace.

As you cutback, you have more and more time between cigarettes. So you will have to do some math. Figure out how many hours you are awake a day. Then keep in mind the number of cigarettes you are allowed for that day according to the easy way. Say you have 20 cigarettes allowed for the day and you are awake 16 hours a day. You multiply 60 x 16 and you get 960.

Then divide 960 by 20 and you get 48. That means you can smoke 1 cigarette every 48 minutes for the day.

Use the pages that follow this chapter to keep track of your progress. If you smoke 20 cigarettes a day, start day one 19.This part of the book will help if you forget how many cigarettes you are allowed for the day when you wake up. Just look at your book. If you mess up and smoke more than your supposed to on one day just go back to the original plan and smoke what you are allowed the following day.

If you smoke more than forty cigarettes a day you can still start with 39 in the book. You will have a withdrawal period but it will be worth it to quit smoking in a shorter period of time. Or you can use your calender to track your progress. Just mark each day of your calender with the number of cigarettes allowed until you get to one.

The first day you go without a cigarette will be much easier than cold turkey because you have cut down gradually while getting use to less and less nicotine.

Okay now you are finished. Your last cigarette was yesterday. What do you do if you have a nicotine craving? Chew Big Red (cinnamon) gum, of course. Don't chew the gum until you have completely quit smoking. Why? Well it's something to look forward to. It should not be used in conjunction with smoking because it defeats the purpose of stopping the cravings.

Of course you can chew the cinnamon gum if you really think you need to before you are cigarette free.

Goal
39

_____

Smoked

_____

Reason to Quit #1
I need to quit for my health.

Goal
38

_____

Smoked

_____

Reason to Quit #2.
A good reason to quit is so I won't burn holes in my car anymore.

Goal
37

_____

Smoked

_____

Reason to Quit #3.

I should quit so I can sit in non-smoking or smoking sections in a restaurant.

Goal
36

Smoked

Reason to Quit #4.
I want a better spiritual life.

Goal
35

Smoked

Reason to Quit #5.
I want my spouse to be pleased with me.

Goal 34

Smoked

Reason to Quit #6.
My clothes smell like smoke.

Goal
33

_____

Smoked

_____

Reason to Quit #7.
My hair smells like smoke.

Goal
32

Smoked

Reason to Quit #8.
I want fresh breath.

Goal
31

Smoked

Reason to Quit #9.
My car smells like smoke.

Goal

30

Smoked

Reason to Quit #10.
I'm sick of waiting for a smoke break at work.

Goal
29

_____

Smoked

_____

Reason to Quit #11.
I don't want to be out of breath while hiking.

Goal
28

Smoked

Reason to Quit #12.
I'm tired of sitting in class wanting a cigarette
when I should be concentrating.

Goal
27

Smoked

Reason to Quit #13.
I don't want others to breathe in second hand smoke.

Goal 26

Smoked

Reason to Quit #14.
I'll save lots of money.

Goal
25

_____

Smoked

_____

Reason to Quit #15.
A good reason to quit is I'll have more energy.

Goal
24

_____

Smoked

_____

Reason to Quit # 16.
My heart rate and blood pressure will be lower.

Goal
23

_____

Smoked

_____

Reason to Quit #17.
I want to set a good example for my children.

Goal
22

Smoked

Reason to Quit #18.
I will lower my chances of getting a smoking related disease.

Goal
21

Smoked

Reason to Quit #19.
I don't want my face to age faster due to smoking.

Goal
20

Smoked

Reason to Quit # 20.

I don't want more hair on my face caused by smoking.

Goal
19

―――――――――

Smoked

―――――

Reason to Quit #21.
I want to live longer.

Goal 18

Smoked

Reason to Quit #22.
Smoking is ruining my romantic relationship.

Goal
17

_____

Smoked

_____

Reason to Quit #1.
I need to quit for my health.

Goal
16

Smoked

Reason to Quit #2.

A good reason to quit is so I won't burn holes in my car anymore.

Goal
15

_____

Smoked

_____

Reason to Quit #3.
I should quit so I can sit in non-smoking or smoking sections in a restaurant.

Goal 14

Smoked

Reason to Quit #4.
I want a better spiritual life.

Goal
13

Smoked

Reason to Quit #5.
I want my spouse to be pleased with me.

Goal
12

Smoked

Reason to Quit #6.
I want my spouse to be pleased with me.

Goal

11

Smoked

Reason to Quit #6.
My clothes smell like smoke.

Goal
10

Smoked

Reason to Quit #7.
My hair smells like smoke.

Goal

9

Smoked

Reason to Quit #8.
I want fresh breath.

Goal
8

Smoked

Reason to Quit #9.
My car smells like smoke.

Goal
7

————————

Smoked

————

Reason to Quit #10.
I'm sick of waiting for a smoke break at work.

Goal
6

_____

Smoked

_____

Reason to Quit #11.
I don't want to be out of breath while hiking.

Goal
5

Smoked

Reason to Quit #12.

I'm tired of sitting in class wanting a cigarette when I should be concentrating.

Goal
4

Smoked

Reason to Quit#13.
I don't want others to breathe in second hand smoke.

Goal
3

Smoked

Reason to Quit #14.
I'll save lot's of money.

Goal
2

_____

Smoked

▬▬▬▬▬▬

Reason to Quit #15.
A good reason to quit is I'll have more energy.

Goal
1

_____

Smoked

_____

Reason to Quit #16.
My heart rate and blood pressure will be lower.